"DUTY CALLED ME HERE:"
THE SOLDIER COMRADES OF THE
NATIONAL MUSEUM OF THE CIVIL WAR SOLDIER

by
Arthur W. Bergeron, Jr.

TABLE OF CONTENTS

Page

INTRODUCTION

The National Museum of the Civil War Soldier is dedicated to telling the story of the "common" soldiers of the Union and Confederate armies. The basic message of the facility and its exhibits is that, for Northerners and Southerners, the experience of being in the army was much more similar than it was different. Their backgrounds were virtually the same. Most people lived on farms or in small towns. American society was structured at the community level. Few people had traveled very far beyond their immediate area. Americans of the antebellum period had little personal contact with the national government, yet they were well informed about national events and keenly interested in politics. As an example of the latter, eighty-five percent of registered voters turned out for the presidential election of 1860. Americans shared strong beliefs in religion, honor and duty as masculine values, the legacy of the Revolution, and individual responsibility.

Once they joined the armies, men on both sides went through similar experiences. Their uniforms, weapons, and equipment did not differ a great deal, although in time most Northerners wore blue and most Confederates wore gray. Both sides organized their armies the same way. Soldiers had the same kinds of camps, they were drilled by the same military manuals, they ate the same foods, they were paid about the same, and they fought using the same tactics. Of course, the experience of the soldiers diverged slightly as the war progressed. The availability of weapons, equipment, and foodstuffs created subtle, and some not-so-subtle, differences in the soldiers' daily lives.

During the Civil War, approximately 2,000,000 men served in the Union armies, and approximately 900,000 men served in the Confederate armies. Nearly 180,000 black soldiers (known as United States Colored Troops) enlisted in the Union army. Almost five out of every six of those men were former slaves. The South did a much better job of putting men of military age (18-45) into its armies. Almost eighty percent of the South's military pool eventually wore the gray. Only thirty percent of the North's white males of military age served in its armies.

According to *Soldiers Blue and Gray* by noted historian James I. Robertson, Jr., "A typical Civil War soldier was a white, native-born farmer, Protestant, single, and in the 18 to 29 age bracket....Most men of blue and gray were in the 5 feet, 5 inches to 5 feet, 9 inches range." Boys as young as 9 enlisted, most of them serving as musicians, and a few men over the age of 60 appear on some of the muster rolls of the opposing armies. Dozens of nationalities were represented in the ranks of both armies, with Germans and Irish constituting the largest ethnic groups in both armies. Historian James M. McPherson has estimated literacy rates among whites when the war began at

Detail from mural by Keith Rocco

ninety percent in the North and eighty percent in the South. Thus, we are fortunate today to have literally thousands of letters and diaries written by Civil War soldiers that help us understand the day-to-day lives of those men.

The Civil War was the costliest, in terms of soldier deaths, of all the wars in which the United States has fought. In fact, until about mid-way through the Vietnam War, more Americans died in the Civil War than in all other of this country's conflicts combined. Union soldier deaths totaled 334,680. Of that number 110,100 men were killed or mortally wounded in battle. Some 224,580 men died of disease. The numbers for Confederate soldier deaths are harder to determine because of the loss of so many records during the war. An estimated 94,000 men were killed or mortally wounded in battle, and approximately 258,000 men died of disease.

Pamplin Historical Park selected thirteen soldiers as "Comrades" to help guide visitors through the National Museum of the Civil War Soldier. These men represent a balanced cross-section of the nearly 3,000,000 soldiers who fought on both sides between 1861 and 1865. The selection was based upon their residence, civilian occupation, and fate during the conflict. One soldier, Delavan Miller, was picked as a special Comrade for younger visitors. At four places in the exhibits, called Comrade Stations, visitors hear an actor read the actual words—taken from their letters, diaries, or memoirs—of the Soldier Comrade they picked when they entered.

The pages of this booklet contain transcriptions of each Comrade's quotes as heard at each Comrade Station. "Joining Up" describes his motivations for becoming a Civil War soldier. "On the March" describes leaving camp, life on the march, and feelings about going into battle. "A Soldier's Fate" describes his experience in battle, its aftermath, and his return to camp. "A Test of Faith" describes his concerns for those at home and questions defining his continuing commitment to the war.

CHAPTER 1

"JOINING UP"

Why did Southerners and Northerners go to war in 1861, or, more precisely, why did they join the army? Historians have discussed many reasons, but those can be boiled down to a few main ones. First and foremost, men on both sides of the Mason and Dixon Line felt that their values and way of life were threatened by the other side. This can be called patriotism. Virtually every historian who has studied the common soldier has commented on the importance of the legacy of the American Revolution in motivating them to fight. Perhaps Professor James M. McPherson said it best in his book *What They Fought For, 1861-1865*:

"These themes of liberty and republicanism formed the ideological core of the cause for which Civil War soldiers fought,...Americans in both North and South believed themselves custodians of the legacy of 1776. The crisis of 1861 was the great test of whether they were worthy of the heritage of liberty bequeathed to them by the founding fathers...."

"The profound irony of the Civil War was that Confederate and Union soldiers...interpreted the heritage of 1776 in opposite ways. Confederates fought for liberty and independence from what they regarded as a tyrannical government; Unionists fought to preserve the nation created by the founders from dismemberment and destruction...."

It is hard to overestimate the role that values like honor and duty played in causing men to enlist. To quote Reid Mitchell, "Fighting was a man's responsibility—if one did not fight one was less than a man. Men may very well have fought during the Civil War for reasons having less to do with ideology than with masculine identity." In the South, the code of honor was perhaps stronger than in the North. It went hand-in-hand with Southerners' perception of liberty or freedom. To most Southern men, it was better to lose their lives than to lose their honor. A man without honor was no man at all.

Detail from mural by Keith Rocco

Another cause was much stronger for Southerners than it was for Northerners—the protection of their homes and families. Though of divided opinions on the subject of secession, the probability of invasion by Northern armies united Southerners. They might argue against the breakup of the Union, but they resented Northerners trying to tell them what to do. Invasion was seen as a threat to each community, and most Southerners moved to try to stop it. Only after the war began and Confederate armies conducted raids into the North did men there feel their homes and families threatened.

Only a handful of white men joined the armies with the thought of either destroying or defending slavery. The great majority of Union soldiers opposed freeing the slaves, although as the war progressed they saw emancipation as a means of weakening the South and bringing the war to a swifter conclusion. For the approximately 180,000 blacks who joined the Union armies, however, the goal of freedom for all slaves was their primary motivation for enlisting.

GEORGE WASHINGTON BEIDELMAN

George Washington Beidelman, from a German family in Bloomsburg, Pennsylvania, became a printer in Philadelphia before the war. On May 21, 1861, at age twenty-two, he enlisted as a private in Company C, 71st Pennsylvania Infantry, which saw duty around Washington, D. C., and later joined the Union Army of the Potomac. Beidelman's enlistment papers described him as 5 feet 9 1/2 inches tall, with a sandy complexion, grey eyes, and sandy hair.

"Shall we…fold our arms and look with satisfaction and indifference until the vile worm of secession and treason has eaten out the very heart of our country's greatness…? Although

Private George Washington Beidelman.

Courtesy United States Army Military History
Institute, Carlisle Barracks, Pennsylvania.

willing to grant favors, I do not believe in acceding to the modest request of Mr. Jeff Davis, to be 'let alone.' He and his allies have been 'let alone' much too long already, and that is why the loyal citizens of the government now find it necessary to shoulder their muskets in defense of their own liberties and those of their children. This contest is not the North against the South; it is government against anarchy, law against disorder, Union against disunion, and truth and justice against falsehood and intolerance. I do not see how any one with a spark of patriotism could hesitate what stand to take, or what cause to espouse."

HENRY ROBINSON BERKELEY

Henry Robinson Berkeley, twenty-one-year-old son of a prominent planter family in Hanover County, Virginia, was known to his family and friends as "Robin." On May 17, 1861, he left Hanover Academy to enlist in the Hanover Battery, which was stationed at Yorktown and became a part of the Confederate Army of Northern Virginia. When his battery was disbanded in October, 1862, Berkeley joined Captain Thomas J. Kirkpatrick's Amherst (Virginia) Artillery.

"Parents and sisters tried hard to be bright and cheerful for their soldier-boys' sakes, but it was impossible for them to hide their deep anxiety....We all went up to [my home] to take supper and bid them good-by. Sad and anxious-looking faces greeted us; but warm and tender hearts bade us good-by, doubtless praying that God would watch over us and soon bring us back in peace and safety.

"...[We] are ready to measure strength with these vile Yanks. I don't see why they don't go home and leave us alone. That is all we ask. But here they are with a vile mercenary army, burning our towns, destroying our crops, desolating our country and killing our people. I wish all the Yanks and all the Negroes were in Africa."

CHARLES BRANDEGEE

Charles Brandegee, a sixteen-year-old student from Berlin, Connecticut, was about five feet, five-and-a-half inches tall, with dark hair and gray eyes. He enlisted on January 11, 1862, in New York City as a private in Company I, 5th New York Infantry, a regiment in the Union Army of the Potomac also known as "Duryee's Zouaves."

"So you see the matter is all fixed and I am booked in Uncle Sam's service for three years in the war. Rest assured I shall do my best and never disgrace the immortal name of Brandegee. Therefore I want you all to write me as cheerful letters as possible and I shall do the same....Tell Mother to cheer up. I am not troubled. I am here by my own will and I am willing to take the consequences. I shall do my best as I always have done. If I am killed I shall be out of misery. If I am wounded I can perhaps get my discharge with honorable scars, and if I serve eighteen more months, why I do. Don't worry at home, don't for my sake."

Private Henry Robinson Berkeley.

Courtesy Virginia Historical Society,
Richmond, Virginia.

WILLIAM BULL

William Bull was born in Shelbyville, Kentucky. When the war began he was a student in St. Louis, Missouri. He enlisted April 30, 1861, as an eighteen-year-old private in a pro-Confederate militia company, then in a company of the Missouri State Guard. Bull later became a private in Captain Charles B. Lesueur's Missouri Battery, which served in General Sterling Price's Confederate army in the Trans-Mississippi Department. Before the war ended, Bull was promoted to the rank of sergeant.

"This question of coercion caused an immediate realignment of parties, and many...who had earnestly desired the preservation of the Union, when it came to a question of coercion, aligned themselves on the side of the South."

"…War between the sections seeming inevitable, I determined to join a military company and receive the instruction which would fit me to fight for the South."

"…Our parting from friends would have been sadder could they and we have foreseen the years that would intervene before meeting again and the dangers and hardships that would fill those years. But could all this have been known, I do not think it would have deterred one from doing what he considered his patriotic duty. We were in high spirits particularly when we left."

VALERIUS CINCINNATUS GILES

Valerius Cincinnatus Giles, a nineteen-year-old farmer from near Austin, Texas, did not have much formal education but was an avid reader. He enlisted in the "Tom Green Rifles," which was mustered into Confederate service on July 11, 1861, and later became Company B, 4th Texas Infantry. That unit was part of John Bell Hood's famous Texas Brigade of the Confederate Army of Northern Virginia.

"[My comrades and I] were representative men from all portions of the state—young, impetuous and fresh, full of energy, enterprise, and fire—… men who, when they first heard the shrill shriek of battle as it came from the far-off coast of South Carolina, at once ceased to argue as to the whyfores and the wherefores—it was enough to know the struggle had commenced, and that they were Southerns."

"...Some came in from the far-off frontier. Some came down from the hills of the North, and some came up from the savannas of the South.... Among them could be found men of all trades and professions,...all for the time being willing to lay aside their plans of personal ambition, and to place themselves on the altar of their country, under the leveling discipline of the army."

GEORGE JOB HUNTLEY

George Job Huntley was a twenty-year-old farmer from Rutherford County, North Carolina. Family tradition states that he also did some teaching. On November 10, 1861, Huntley enlisted as a musician in the "Rutherford Band," which was mustered in as Company I, 34th North Carolina Infantry. The unit saw service in its home state until April, 1862, when it went to Richmond and became part of the Confederate Army of Northern Virginia. Huntley was promoted to sergeant and then third lieutenant of his company.

"I am unable to tell what will be the result of this war. This much I can say, I don't want to hear tell of any Union flag being raised anywhere in the South until we know the terms that we are going back in the Union on....I have always enjoyed Liberty, and if I can't enjoy it through life I expect my bones to rest in the grave....They may gain victories here and there, but that will not dishearten those that expect to have liberty. If they will not give us our liberty as a free people, we will fall back and fight them at every creek, river, and town from here to the Blue Ridge."

ELI PINSON LANDERS

Eli Pinson Landers, a twenty-one-year-old farmer from Gwinnett County, Georgia, was devoutly religious, the grandson of a Baptist minister. On August 11, 1861, he joined the "Flint Hill Grays," which was mustered into service as Company H, 16th

Georgia Infantry. Private Landers and his unit traveled by train to Richmond, Virginia, and later joined the Confederate Army of Northern Virginia.

Private Charles Brandegee.

Courtesy Charles B. Livingstone, Calais, Maine.

"Mamma, I want to see you and Caroline the worst you ever saw!...But don't you study about me, for if I am called to the field I hope that I will come out unhurt, but if I never see old Gwinnett, let my post stand. Tell Miss Cody that I was glad I have got out of her cotton patch!"

"...I hope that the day will come when it will not be in dreams that I will be with you, when we will set down 'round your table to eat in independent peace, for that is the only way that I ever expect to eat with you again. My dear Mother, it is a dreadful life but I feel reconciled to it, for I believe that we are on the right side of the question."

DELAVAN S. MILLER

Delavan S. Miller was a 13-year-old resident of West Carthage, New York, when the Civil War began. In March 1862, he enlisted in the Morgan Flying Artillery, which was Company H, 2nd New York Heavy Artillery. His father (a widower) served as a sergeant in that company and did not know that Delavan had joined the unit until the lad reported at the regiment's camp near Washington, D. C. Because of his age, Delavan became a drummer for the regiment. The 2nd New York Heavy Artillery saw duty in the Washington defenses and later joined the Union Army of the Potomac.

"When the news was flashed across the country that Fort Sumter had been fired upon, I was a twelve-year-old boy....Favorite sports and pastimes lost their zest. Juvenile military companies paraded the streets every evening, and make-believe battles were fought every Saturday afternoon."

"After the regiment was sent to Virginia, Captain Smith...returned home after more men. He brought a letter to me from my father and, patting me on my head, asked me in a joking way how I would like to be a soldier....I pleaded with the officer to take me back with him. My mother was dead, my home was broken up; I argued that I would be better off with my father."

"The tender-hearted captain sympathized with me, but said he did not know what he could do with such a little fellow. I would not be put off, however....After much begging, the captain said that...he would try to take me back with him."

"In March, 1862, when two months past thirteen years old, I started for the war with a squad of recruits."

ALEXANDER HERRITAGE NEWTON

Alexander Herritage Newton was born in New Berne, North Carolina, to a slave father and free mother—his mother's status made him a free man. Newton became a cook on a steamer and

Sergeant William Jeffery Bull.

Courtesy Missouri Historical Society, St. Louis.

left North Carolina for New York City in July 1857. There on June 16, 1859, he married Olivia A. Hamilton. On December 18, 1863, at age twenty-four, he enlisted in Company E, 29th Connecticut Infantry, and was soon promoted to commissary sergeant. After service in Beaufort, South Carolina, his regiment moved to Virginia in August 1864, becoming part of the Union Army of the James.

"Inspired with the thought of Shakespeare, who said, 'He who would be free, let him first strike the blow himself,' my bosom burned with the fire of patriotism for the salvation of my country and the freedom of my people. ..."

"The regiment paraded the streets while multitudes looked with wonder, some laughing, others cheering,...as they marched away to do battle for the noblest of causes....Mother, father, wife and children, ladies and gentlemen of my friends, both white and black, were bidding me good bye....I cannot express the sobbing emotions of my heart, when I ungrasped the hands of these loved ones and friends...knowing that I might be going to my death and never again see them in this world."

WILLIAM CHARLES HENRY REEDER

William Charles Henry Reeder, a twenty-one-year-old cabinet maker from Peru, Ohio, enlisted in July 1861 as a private in Company A, 20th Indiana Infantry. He and his comrades remained in camp for several months before receiving weapons or uniforms. After brief service on the North Carolina coast, the regiment moved to Virginia, becoming part of the Union Army of the Potomac.

"I do not want you to think I was scared into it, for I was not—it was an act of my own free will, and I hope you will sanction it with all your heart. …"

"…I am very well satisfied with my lot, as much so as could be expected of a person changing his living so much as I did. …"

"I sometimes think I would like to come home, but when I get to thinking how folks would talk about me a'backing out, I then have no thoughts of coming home then."

"As the Preacher said today, I will...acquit myself like a man, not like a coward or deserter....And if it is my lot to fall, you will have the assurance that it was in a good cause. But I have no fears of that."

ELISHA STOCKWELL, JR.

Elisha Stockwell, Jr., was born in Massachusetts, but his family moved to Wisconsin in 1849. He became a farmer in Jackson County. In February 1862, at age fifteen, Stockwell enlisted as a private in Company I, 14th Wisconsin Infantry. This regiment engaged in a number of battles in the war's Western Theater as part of the Union Army of the Tennessee. Near the end of the war, Stockwell was promoted to the rank of corporal.

"My father was there and objected to my going, so they scratched my name out, which humiliated me somewhat. My sister gave me a severe calling down the first time I saw her for exposing my ignorance before the public, and called me a 'little snotty boy,' which raised my anger. I told her, 'Never mind, I'll go and show you that I am not the little boy you think I am.' …"

"…The captain got me in by my lying a little, as I told the recruiting officer I didn't know just how old I was but thought I was eighteen. He didn't measure my height, but called me five feet, five inches high. I wasn't that tall two years later when I re-enlisted, but they let it go."

"I enlisted the twenty-fifth of February, 1862, and got my uniform."

PETER WELSH

Peter Welsh was born to Irish parents living in Canada. He moved to Boston in the 1850s and became a carpenter. He married Margaret Prendergast of Charlestown, Massachusetts, and they moved to New York City. On September 3, 1862, at age thirty two, Welsh enlisted as a private in Company K, 28th Massachusetts Infantry—part of the Union Army of the Potomac's famous "Irish Brigade." Welsh eventually received promotion to the rank of sergeant.

"This is my country as much as the man that was born on the soil, and so it is with every man who comes to this country and becomes a citizen. This being the case, I have as much interest in the maintenance of the government and laws and integrity of the nation as any other man....This war, with all its evils, with all its errors and mismanagement, is a war in which the people of all nations have a vital interest. This is the first test of a modern free government in the act of sustaining itself against internal enemies and matured rebellion....What would be the condition today of hundreds of thousands of the sons and daughters of poor oppressed old Erin if they had not a free land like this to emigrate to?"

Detail from mural by Keith Rocco

WILLIAM MARCUS WOODCOCK

William Marcus Woodcock was a nineteen-year-old student from Macon County, Tennessee. In September, 1861, he enlisted as a private in Company B, 9th Kentucky Infantry. This regiment became a part of the Union Army of the Ohio, renamed the Army of the Cumberland in late 1862. Company records describe Woodcock as five feet, eleven inches tall, with gray eyes and fair complexion. He received promotions several times, ending the war as a second lieutenant.

"I was aroused from my slumber a little after sunrise and ate the last breakfast that I ate as a citizen....Oh, God! had I known what was in store for me, I could not have endured the thought of it. For a citizen's idea of soldiering is that it is ten-fold more dangerous and difficult to follow than it really is, and that man cannot endure such a great amount of fatigue and destitution as he really can. ..."

"...I meditated deeply on the question: Am I risking too much when I enter the army?...I had many reasons for wishing to stay out of the army (besides the natural one of dread). I had many connections that it would almost rend my heart to break off."

CHAPTER 2

"ON THE MARCH"

Civil War soldiers naturally felt a little uncertain as they left camp to begin active campaigning and when they went into battle. Life on the march sometimes was hard—soldiers had to tramp great distances over poor roads in all kinds of weather, often with poorly made or fitted footware. Early in the war, soldiers were out of shape and not used to walking such long distances. They became much better marchers as the war progressed and could easily cover a dozen miles in a day. Some marches covered much longer distances, as many as 30 miles.

The march was slow (about 2.5 miles per hour) as huge numbers of men, horses, wagons, and artillery moved across

Detail from mural by Keith Rocco

poor roads into unfamiliar, and possibly hostile, territory. Often there were wrong turns and doubling back due to poor maps. Dirt roads were quickly torn up by animals, wagons, and artillery; when conditions permitted, the soldiers marched along side of the road, not on it. Men in the rear suffered from the dust stirred up by the head of the column. Accordion-like starts and stops added to the soldier's frustration. Stragglers were a constant problem. Men who were hungry or thirsty might drop out of the column; others simply left to plunder nearby houses and farms. Illness or the lack of good shoes caused many to straggle.

Soldiers who were about to encounter the enemy for the first time wondered how they would perform when called to battle. Inwardly, each man prepared for the coming clash in his own way, wondering whether he would stand his ground, or be killed—and whether he could kill, if called upon to do so. Waiting in line of battle caused minutes to seem like hours. To pass the time, soldiers might pray or read their Bibles. Others swore loudly that they would never again curse, gamble, or drink if they were spared. Fear affected soldiers in many ways—dry mouth and throat, sweating, stomach spasms, and even hyperventilation. Most men feared showing cowardice more than being killed or wounded.

GEORGE WASHINGTON BEIDELMAN

"Heigh ho! there goes the bugle, which means 'fall in.'… On the march at last. The road is so crowded that we can get along but slowly....On the way we came across some fine cornfields, and the way the green corn had to suffer is a caution. It is the first the boys have had this season....It would be amusing to you to see us all rush to get fires made and cook our meals. Each one carries his own rations and cooks his own mess. …"

"…Our march today was tedious, but not very hard; the weather is cool enough, but the dust is almost intolerable. ... It is in most places like wading through the snow in winter. We eat dust, drink dust, breathe dust, and are thoroughly filled and covered with it from head to foot. It will take us about a week to get clean after our march. …"

"… When the order to move against the enemy's position was issued, how quickly did all our fond anticipations vanish!..."

"…The Rebels are in plain sight. May the Lord be with us and protect us, and give the victory. My trust is in Him. …"

HENRY ROBINSON BERKELEY

"We continued our march....We had very little to eat, our commissary wagons being stuck in the mud, and many being compelled to throw out the rations in order to get along. John Lewis and I got hold of some corn, and parched and ate it. …"

"…After getting within a mile of Warrenton, our horses gave entirely out, and our company was left behind with orders to rest our horses one day and then to follow the command. …"

"…We started again in wind, rain, and utter darkness, and men and horses were floundering the whole of that night. And when daylight came, we had only gotten about a mile or two from camp, while men and horses were worn out and little fit for a hard day's march over a heavy and muddy road."

"The Yankees appeared in our front early this morning...and began shelling us....This was the first time I was under fire, and I thought we would all be killed. However, no one was hurt, not even a horse. Their small rifle shells did us no harm, bursting harmlessly above our heads and the fragments going far in our rear."

CHARLES BRANDEGEE

"It is awful work, this marching on a hot day over rough roads with all a man's effects on his back. I have seen soldiers drop down in the road and stay there till picked up by the ambulance....I have the reputation of being some on a march and, indeed, I have never lagged behind yet."

"…We started in reality at three o'clock, marching about two miles. Then we...formed into divisions and halted at the edge of a patch of woods to wait for the trains of the preceding divisions to go by...."

Private Valerius Cincinnatus Giles.

Courtesy Lawrence T. Jones, Austin, Texas.

"...It commenced to rain, and we only went about a quarter mile more before our brigade encamped for the night in a large wood close by the road. In a few minutes, large fires were blazing in all directions, and the men set to work building shelters, cooking coffee, etcetera...."

"Oh! what roads!...In addition to the rain and...frost, the passage of perhaps seventy or eighty pieces of artillery...and the ammunition, pontoons, and ambulance trains had made it, to use a mild expression, 'perfectly awful.'"

"I hope the ball will open before long, for I am tired of expecting it."

WILLIAM BULL

"My brother John, Dave Holliday, and I drove on the same gun—John in the lead, I in the swing, and Dave the wheeler....The weather was intensely cold,...and it was probably the hardest experience we had during the war, being, as we were, in that transition stage from the easy and comfortable life of the civilian to the life of the soldier, which is full of hardships and privations."

"Reveille was sounded before daylight, when we had to rise, dress in the cold, attend roll call, feed and curry our horses— then get our soldiers' breakfast of bacon, hardtack, and black coffee, which, while it would have been considered most sumptuous later in our experience, seemed poor indeed to us so recently from our good eating at home."

"After breakfast 'boots and saddles' would be sounded, when we would have to put the heavy artillery harness, which had become frozen during the night, on the horses and prepare for the march, which was resumed at daylight. Many of us had hands and feet frost-bitten, but we were cheerful under it all, feeling that no sacrifice, even to the loss of life, was too great for the Cause."

VALERIUS CINCINNATUS GILES

"We had now traveled a distance of one hundred fifty-five miles in a period of about twelve days. During this entire period we had seen but one dry day, and the men had not known what it was to have dry clothing or dry bedding. On the march during the day, they were wholly unprotected from the peltings of the elements, and at night threw themselves on the wet ground, very frequently without fires, where they shivered the night through."

"In order to travel better, the men divested themselves of all heavy articles of apparel, even to their coats, pants, and shoes. It was a common spectacle on the road to see a manly specimen of human nature trudging along singing 'Dixie' as he went, minus everything in the shape of clothes except a shirt. …"

"…The artillery and supply trains preceded the infantry and left the narrow roads in a horrible condition. The mud was deep and cold, and our progress was necessarily slow."

"…How little did we dream of our fate. Hope never deserts a soldier, though death may stare him in the face. It is a glorious thing that the unknown future is concealed from us."

Lieutenant George Job Huntley.

Courtesy Mrs. Jo Allman, Winston-Salem, North Carolina.

GEORGE JOB HUNTLEY

"I am very unwell at this time, caused, I suppose, by so much hard marching and exposure. We have been marching nearly constant day and night for three weeks past, and there has been a power of rain and we have taken it all. Just lie down and lie in the rain all night without anything over us. …"

"We have got orders now to cook two day's rations to move somewhere, I reckon, but I don't know where....We threw out our pickets and was ordered to lie down on our guns. and no man to offer to sleep one wink....The night was clear and nice. Everything was calm except the occasional firing of the pickets. The whippoorwill hollered all night. The moon shone brightly while we was lying there in that position, only waiting, it seemed like, for the sun to rise to march out to meet death....Oh how many in the course of twenty-four hours would exchange time for eternity. Stop for a moment, if you please, and think of such a condition. I felt like that I would be much better satisfied if I knew my friends was praying in my behalf."

ELI PINSON LANDERS

"We have had a long, hard march since I wrote you last and some very hot weather....There was hundreds of our boys fainted and fell in the road, and many of them died. But I have been able to keep up all the way....Us soldiers treats the people with respects when we want anything, and we offer them our money for it—and if they refuse it we just take it at our own price. ..."

"...The dust in the roads is shoe-mouth deep. When marching, the dust rises so thick a person can hardly see his way."

"...You heard a false tale about me starting to a battle and giving out. It is very true I did not get to the battle, but I got as far as any of the rest did. We thought we was going into a fight, but the enemy did not come out to face the music. They say that they are fighting at the place we are going to....My dear Mother, if I never meet you again and should meet the dead fate of some of my friends, I hope to meet you in a world of peace and pleasure."

DELAVAN S. MILLER

"Late that afternoon we started out on the road...and were rushed along at a lively walk until nearly midnight. The men were young and lighthearted, and as we marched there were laughs, jokes, and weird and humorous sayings breaking out from the ranks here and there, and then all would sing 'John Brown's Body' and 'We'll Hang Jeff Davis to a Sour Apple Tree.'"

"[T]here had been much discussion among the musicians as to what we would do in case of a battle. No instructions had been given us, and we had rather come to the conclusion among ourselves that when we got to close quarters, we would drop out and keep as much out of range as possible."

"Our nervousness...increased as we approached the front. Occasionally some of the boys would suggest to...our drum major that it was about time for us to fall out. There was 'no use of us going up to get shot at when we had nothing to shoot back with.'"

ALEXANDER HERRITAGE NEWTON

"On...an oppressively hot day, we marched into Virginia. We were worn out, weary, thirsty, hungry, and completely exhausted. We were compelled to carry our blankets, knapsack, musket, and sixty rounds of cartridges. About 4 PM we reached the woods and encamped. I was so overcome with the heat that I fell to the ground and was soon asleep...."

"We had for our dinner, breakfast, and supper, half-done salt pork, which was placed on a stick and held over a blaze to warm it; hard tack, on which one could hardly make an impression with the teeth, and sometimes coffee. ..."

"...The troops were ordered to prepare two days' rations and to get ready for light marching. I had opportunity now to be in the company of commissioned officers for a few hours at a time, when we halted for rest....I somehow had the feeling that something was going on, or was going to happen, that would require one to be wise and cunning—...and in fact all the field officers seemed to be uneasy. Three o'clock one morning, my surmises were justified, for the long roll was sounded, and soon we were in line for work."

WILLIAM CHARLES HENRY REEDER

"We are all packed and ready to go at any moment....The whole regiment is in an uproar:...everyone delighted at the idea of getting away from here, and that there is some chance of having a fight. …"

"They put us through so on the march that we were pretty well used up. The regiments in front of us threw their knapsacks, every man of them, and put a guard over them, and after they got into town, they got teams and went and fetched them....On arriving here I pulled my boots, and my feet were all in blisters— … they did not hurt me while I was a'going, but the next morning I was like a foundered horse....We had nothing but hard crackers to eat for two days, so we felt pretty lank."

Private Eli Pinson Landers.

Courtesy Dr. Elizabeth W. Roberson,
Williamston, North Carolina.

"…Should we get into a fight, I will do my best. And if I fall, I want my face to be to the enemy. And if I am spared through the battle,...I think the fighting will be over, and I may stand a chance of returning home safe once more....Rest easy—you shall hear from me often, or as long as I am able to write."

ELISHA STOCKWELL, JR.

"We were soon ready to go. We rolled our blankets up (each had a wool and oilcloth blanket), with the oilcloth on the outside, tied the two ends together, and put the roll over our heads and across the left shoulder, took our canteens and haversack, and left the camp in charge of the men that were on the sick list and excused from duty."

"...There was lots of foraging on this march, and houses burned. The fences on both sides of the road...were on fire in places."

"...Our cartridge box was inspected three times a day, and if a cartridge was missing, it was fifty cents, and ten dollars for killing a hog, to be taken out of the next payroll...."

"[When we reached the battle,] the first dead man we saw was...leaning back against a big tree as if asleep, but his intestines were all over his legs and several times their natural size....I know my face was as white as anyone's,...and I thought what a foolish boy I was to run away to get into such a mess as I was in. I would have been glad to have seen my father coming after me."

PETER WELSH

"We started [next morning] and marched all day until dark. The day was very hot, and the dust was suffocating....Next morning we started at eight o'clock and marched. There was hundreds of men who had to fall out of the ranks and stay behind. The weather was so hot and we were on a forced march...."

"...We arrived after making four forced marches. The last day it was raining and the roads were bad, which made marching purty hard....Halted about a mile from the ferry and pitched tents just at dark. Got orders to strike tents, and started for the ferry.

There was so many troops to cross that it was midnight when we got into a field about a mile on this side of the river, where we lay down for the night."

"...In hot weather you do not know what a treat it is to a man here to get some milk or a bit of butter, when they have been weeks and months, perhaps, without tasting anything but hard bread and salt pork and coffee, with once in a while a little fresh beef. No vegetables. Nothing but the same old thing over and over again."

WILLIAM MARCUS WOODCOCK

"We pulled up stakes and moved toward the front....Every day we could hear cannons booming from each wing of the Army.... An order had been received to cause the men to leave their knapsacks with the wagons, and to carry only their haversack, canteen, and blanket, besides guns and accouterments, and the indications were that active operations would immediately commence."

"These little marches wearied me very much, and I scarcely now can conceive how I mustered resolution to put a good face upon matters as I did, when I was suffering to such extent from mental and physical sickness and fatigue."

"Oh, how can I portray the anguish of mind the soldier suffers while he is waiting in dread expectation of a battle! What were my feelings as I calculated the chances that I felt I would certainly have of being a bloody and mangled corpse before night?...If I should live, how many of my comrades had spent their last happy hour on the earth, and with whom I had spent my last agreeable moment? I endured such heart-rending thoughts as these till I actually prayed for the battle to begin, for then one has no time for meditation."

CHAPTER 3

"A SOLDIER'S FATE"

Most soldiers survived battle and remained with their units physically unscathed. Those that did not met one of three fates: killed or mortally wounded, wounded, or taken prisoner by the enemy. Averaged over the war as a whole, a soldier's chance of being killed or mortally wounded in battle was about one in sixty. Battlefields became graveyards, and burial duty was nearly as horrifying as the battle itself. Bodies remained on the field until overworked burial parties could find them all. In siege situations, truces were arranged for burial parties to begin work. Often, large temporary graves were created with the intention of later individual re-burial under more calm circumstances. Soldiers feared an anonymous death and burial, and they frequently sewed inside their uniforms pieces of paper on which they had written their name and unit. They hoped that, if they fell, a comrade might thus be able to mark their graves.

The chances of being wounded were about one in eight. Soldiers survived these wounds either because of or in spite of field medical practices that were struggling to keep up with the capacity to inflict injury. The wounded experienced not only pain but thirst as well. They might lie on the battlefield for hours or even days before being found and taken to a field hospital. Even then, hours might pass before they received treatment. After treatment in the field, many wounded soldiers were sent to permanent hospitals to recuperate. Many of these hospitals were excellent, but soldiers still succumbed to infection because doctors did not understand its cause and had no medicines to prevent or treat it.

A soldier's chances of being captured were about one in thirteen. At times during the war, soldiers were "paroled" upon their promise not to take up arms until "exchanged" for prisoners from the other side. An official system was established in 1862 whereby the two sides exchanged (traded) prisoners of war. Most men captured, however, were sent to prisoner of war camps scattered around both countries. In most cases, these facilities were poorly prepared to house, feed, and care for the men.

Detail from mural by Keith Rocco

Soldiers in prison camps had to endure limited food, poor sanitation, erratic administration, and disease. Escape was possible, but the successful traversing of miles of unfamiliar enemy territory was accomplished by few. Many soldiers did not survive their captivity. Both Union and Confederate prisoners suffered as victims of disease and malnutrition, and about 13.7 percent died.

GEORGE WASHINGTON BEIDELMAN

"Reveille long before daylight, with orders to make our coffee, and be ready to march in an hour....We advanced in regular line of battle, the shells dropping amongst us as thick as need be, but not doing much damage....The wounded were taken off as fast as possible.... We were hotly engaged for a short time, and our regiment suffered considerably.... This is my first big battle, and so far—the Lord be praised—I am still unharmed."

"At dark firing has nearly ceased, and we hold our position and sleep on our arms all night. I do not know the result of today's battle. About sunset a comrade and myself started to take a view of the field in the immediate vicinity, and oh! what sickening sights! Nearly all of our own men have been collected and buried, but there lie the Rebels yet just as they fell, in all shapes and positions....We must have seen four or five hundred in a space of that many yards square; and recollect the line of battle was five or six miles long. The bodies are all swelled, turned black, and mortifying, and the stench is becoming almost unendurable."

HENRY ROBINSON BERKELEY

"On reaching the...swamp, we found the Yanks on the opposite side in line of battle, ready to dispute our passage. Our battery with four others, making about thirty cannon, were soon put in position...and were very hotly engaged for about three hours. We lost no men but had four horses killed. I can't see how we escaped. ..."

"...A cannon ball came very near taking my head off today....I was leaning over aiming my cannon and it passed just over my head. If I had been standing up it would have struck me full in the face."

"...We went over the battlefield yesterday evening, where knapsacks, haversacks, oilcloths, blankets, and plunder of every description lay thick....I secured two oilcloths and a beautiful red blanket. ..."

"...The doctors established the field hospital of the First and Second divisions at a spring near us, and very soon they began to bring out the wounded....It is a beautiful spring day on which all this bloody work is being done.... This morning when I got up about 4 AM there was a big pile of amputated arms, hands, legs, and fingers within a foot or two of me. A horrid sight."

CHARLES BRANDEGEE

In May 1863, after his regiment was disbanded, Charles Brandegee re-enlisted as a private in Company A, 146th New York Infantry. On the afternoon of May 5, 1864, at the Battle of the Wilderness, Virginia, this regiment attacked across Saunders' Field near the Orange Turnpike, and engaged with troops of Major General Edward Johnson's Confederate division. They quickly found themselves surrounded, their line of retreat severed. Brandegee was captured with several hundred members of his regiment. A fellow soldier wrote Brandegee's father to tell him of his son's capture:

"He stood on the right of me when we were surrounded and ordered to surrender. But part of us broke the Rebel line, and in that way a great many of us got away, although a great many was taken prisoner."

WILLIAM BULL

"We had to pass in rear of and along the entire length of the Brigade, which was in line and fighting most desperately with the enemy.... The cannoneers and drivers were permitted to dismount and shield themselves as much as possible behind the carriages and the horses,...but the officers and sergeants had to remain mounted and set a good example to the men by appearing to be indifferent to danger. I don't know how it was with the others, but I found it very difficult to avoid ducking when the balls seemed to come very close to my head. ..."

"...While two of our pieces...were firing rapidly,...Larrie Gilespie, acting as Number One on one of the Guns, thinking his gun had been fired, stepped in to sponge out just as the lanyard was pulled to fire his gun. His arms and the front of his skull was blown off, but he was still alive when we left the field the following day. We left him with great regret in the...Tavern, where he was moved soon after the unfortunate accident."

"...My brother John looked me up after the battle, and we were rejoiced to find that neither had been injured."

VALERIUS CINCINNATUS GILES

"The advance lines of the two armies in many places were not more than fifty yards apart. Everything was on the shoot. No favors asked, and none offered."

"My gun was so dirty that the ramrod hung in the barrel, and I could neither get it down nor out. I...drove home ramrod, cartridge, and all, laid the gun on a boulder, elevated the muzzle, ducked my head, holloaed 'Look out!' and pulled the trigger. She roared like a young cannon and flew over my boulder. ..."

"...Fifty yards from the crest of the hill I suddenly stopped,

Private Delavan S. Miller.

Courtesy United States Army Military History Institute,
Carlisle Barracks, Pennsylvania.

knocked out completely by grapeshot. Hundreds of men passed me, yelling, shouting, and swearing. As I lay there in an open space, unable to move, exposed to a terrific fire,...a stalwart fellow...in passing grabbed me by the collar of my coat and unceremoniously snaked me along for a few yards and landed me behind a big apple tree. He handled me without gloves and hurt me fearfully, and in return for that act of humanity I cursed him. He made no reply, but hurried on with the great wave of victorious soldiers. His name or regiment I never knew, God bless him."

GEORGE JOB HUNTLEY

Lieutenant George Job Huntley, with the rest of his regiment, attacked along the Chambersburg Pike on the afternoon of July 1, 1863, during the Battle of Gettysburg, Pennsylvania. His brigade was attempting to help drive units of the Union First Corps from Seminary Ridge. The North Carolinians came under heavy musket and artillery fire, which devastated their ranks and halted the attack. Huntley was one of the men who went down with severe wounds. He died the following day. In one of his last letters home, George Huntley wrote:

"This may be my last lines to you. If I fall, I want you to spend all my money in sending the children to school."

ELI PINSON LANDERS

"We was about half a mile from the line when the firing commenced.... We did not have time to organize our regiment—we just run in and shot when we had the chance and never formed to line. If a man could get behind a tree it was all right. Some of the boys never fired a gun.... I took two fair pops at them from that tree, but there was so much smoke I could not see whether I killed anyone or not—but I don't know what is the reason for I took deliberate aim at them! The old man was shot right in the forehead but it did not frighten me as bad as I

Sergeant Alexander
Herritage Newton.

From Alexander H. Newton, <u>Out of the
Briars: An Autobiography and Sketch of
the Twenty-ninth Regiment, Connecticut
Volunteers</u> (Miami, Fla.: Mnemosyne
Pub. Co., 1969).

expected it would. But I tell you when the bullets would whistle around my head I felt sort of ticklish."

"…Next morning I went over the battlefield, and it was awful to look at the scene of destruction that had been done. The field was lying thick with our noble Southerners being trampled on."

"…I have saw the wounded hauled off in old four-horse wagons—just throwed in like hogs—some with their legs off, some with their arms off, in terrible conditions."

DELAVAN S. MILLER

"We followed in the rear of the regiment and were halted just under the brow of a hill, where we stood in line nearly two hours. Bullets clipped small branches from the trees, and shells went swishing through the air over our heads. A couple burst in front of us, and an occasional solid shot would go rolling down the hill."

"Probably there is no more difficult situation for troops to be placed in than to be held as a reserve during a battle....If one is going to be shot, it is something of a satisfaction to be able to shoot back. ..."

" [A] few of us hunted up a spring and carried water to our friends....One of the few times that I remember seeing tears in my father's eyes was when I handed him a canteen full of water that morning."

"The fighting continued until well into the night....The surgeons and their helpers worked all night removing the wounded. We carried them out of the woods in blankets."

"Behind our division there were three amputating tables with deep trenches dug at the foot. In the morning those trenches were full of amputated limbs, hands, and fingers, and the piles above the ground were as high as the tables."

ALEXANDER HERRITAGE NEWTON

"We entered into an engagement with the Rebels, and many were wounded, killed, and taken prisoners. I had a very narrow escape:...I remember a twenty-pound cannon ball coming towards me. I could see it distinctly through the smoke. It looked like it had been sent especially for me. I said quickly, 'Lord, you promised that a thousand should fall at my side, but that it should not come nigh me.'...When the ball was within about three feet of me it struck the ground and bounded over my head. God's promise was fulfilled in my case."

"…I stopped where the surgeons were at work. I shall never forget the fearful sight that met my eyes....There were arms and legs piled up like hogs' feet in a butcher shop. The dead and the dying were strewn over the battlefield for miles.... These scenes would have made your heart sore—the wounded and dying scattered over the battlefield thick, the hurrying to and fro of the physicians and the nurses, the prayers and groans and cries of the wounded, the explosions of bombs, the whizzing of bullets, the cracking of rifles; you would have thought that the very forces of hell had been let loose."

Private William Charles Henry Reeder.

Courtesy Craig L. Dunn, Kokomo, Indiana.

WILLIAM CHARLES HENRY REEDER

"We drove them from the woods in the clearing, where they halted.... We made another charge and drove them...in every direction. But they had not far to go until they were in the woods again and were pouring in a deadly fire upon us that was in the clearing.... They were on three sides of us and had us under three cross-fires....[We] would have been taken prisoners if they had not ordered us to fall back. But in the uproar and confusion I did not hear the order, and I stood my ground firing away, when, behold: I looked around and they were all gone.... [I] started off in the direction the rest had taken. But I did not go very far before I got one of their leaden messengers."

"...I am wounded in the right hip and left knee. No bones broken—it is only a flesh wound, and will be well in a short time. We are on our way to Washington, where we will remain until we are well, when we will again join our regiments....I am in good spirits, and my wound is not painful, and grieve not on my account. I will write again shortly."

ELISHA STOCKWELL, JR.

"We stopped,...and I got behind a small tree....The brush was so thick I couldn't see the Rebs, but loaded and fired at the smoke until a grape shot came through the tree and knocked me flat. I thought my arm was gone, but I...couldn't see anything wrong with it, so got to my feet with my gun in my hands. I started to run. At that instant a bullet cut across my right shoulder, and it burned like a red hot iron. My first thought was my clothes were afire. ..."

"I was going all this time, and I began to realize that the Rebs were shooting at me.... I took my place in the front rank, and my left arm began to come to its feeling. It hurt me quite bad, and I...couldn't raise it to my head....At that moment the Lieutenant...asked what was the matter. I showed him where the canister shot had hit my arm—it was halfway between the elbow and shoulder, and had burned the wool on my blouse down to the threads.... The Lieutenant told me to...go to the landing. I was as tickled as a boy let out of school."

PETER WELSH

In the early morning hours of May 12, 1864, during the Battle of Spotsylvania, Virginia, Sergeant Peter Welsh and his regiment attacked a Confederate position nicknamed the "Mule Shoe." The assault was initially successful, and overran the Confederate entrenchments. But then counterattacks stalled the Union drive. Fierce fighting at what became known as "The Bloody Angle" claimed many casualties on both sides, including Peter Welsh, who was wounded. Three days later, he wrote to his wife:

"I have a flesh wound in my left arm—just a nice one to keep me from any more fighting or marching this campaign."

He was transferred to a hospital in Washington, D.C., where surgeons discovered that the bullet had fractured his ulna. They removed the projectile, along with fragments of bone. Welsh improved initially, but then developed a type of blood poisoning. His wife, Margaret, reached his side before he died on May 28, 1864.

WILLIAM MARCUS WOODCOCK

"It was at this point that I heard the first ball whistle from a Rebel gun. It was here that I first saw the ground torn up about my feet by a leaden agent.... And it was here that I first pointed my rifle at a human being and used effort to make my aim so true that it would drive a ball through his brain.... One year previous to this time it would have made me shudder to even see a man through the sights of an empty rifle, but now it was enough for me to know that the man was dressed in gray, and that he was trying to get a shot at some of our boys...—and so I fired away."

After the battle, Marcus Woodcock went to a field hospital to check on some injured comrades.

"Over a thousand maimed, crippled, and otherwise shockingly mangled soldiers had been brought from the battlefield.... Arms and legs, hands and feet, fingers and toes that had just been detached from their quivering stumps were recklessly strewn on every side. Three tables had been continually occupied with subjects for amputation [since] midnight, and continued to be filled for the following two days."

CHAPTER 4

"A TEST OF FAITH"

Having survived difficult campaigns and bloody battles, Civil War soldiers had to decide whether they would continue in military service or be discharged. The soldier faced terrible hardships and fearsome dangers. Why did he go on? If he was motivated by duty, what about his duty to his family? If it was loyalty to his comrades in arms that kept him going, could he trust the new recruits, draftees, substitutes, and bounty men? Was this still his cause...his responsibility?

As the war dragged on, the soldier faced a test of faith. Most renewed their commitment and went on, while some did not. Veterans had no illusions about what reenlistment meant—they were motivated to reenlist out of loyalty to their comrades, commitment to their cause, and belief that victory was achievable. Reenlistment was rewarded with furloughs and bounties.

Many men let their enlistments run out and returned home, feeling that they had discharged their duty. Some men protested bitterly, sometimes to the point of mutiny, if their discharges were even briefly delayed "for the good of the service." Others chose desertion. Some paid for this choice with their lives; others were offered amnesty if they would return to the ranks. Men left to relieve the hardships to their families caused by their long absence, delays in army pay, and the threat of the advancing war. Anti-war sentiment at home, or continuing reverses in the field, led some soldiers to return home at the end of their enlistment or to desert.

GEORGE WASHINGTON BEIDELMAN

On July 3, 1863, Private George Beidelman received a slight wound in both legs at the Battle of Gettysburg. He recovered in a hospital at Chestnut Hill, near Philadelphia, then became post quartermaster sergeant at Camp William Penn, near Chelton Hills, Pennsylvania—an instruction camp for black soldiers that was organized by the state. In early 1864, Beidelman

Detail from mural by Keith Rocco

became ill and wrote to his father:

"I am well, with the exception of a cold in the head—a very common affliction, and one which is always more or less troublesome."

Either his ailment was more "troublesome" than he thought, or it developed into a more serious condition. He died in camp on March 14 of what was termed typhoid pneumonia.

HENRY ROBINSON BERKELEY

Private Henry Robinson Berkeley was captured with thirty-five of his comrades on March 2, 1865, at the Battle of Waynesboro, Virginia. He wrote in his diary:

"I was captured after I had gotten over the railroad bridge in a little piece of oak woods to the left of the railroad as you come east. The Yanks treated us very well. When they overtook us, they simply told us to go to the rear....There were thirty of my company captured with me, and some eight hundred prisoners from the infantry."

Berkeley was imprisoned at Fort Delaware. Nevertheless, he remained committed to his cause.

"I have tried to act as I think for the best interests of my country and my family. These people cannot take from us our liberty without destroying their own. They pretend to make war on us to save the Union—but is a Union pinned together by bayonets worth saving? I think certainly not. We are very near hopeless, and it is not wise for the United States government to render us desperate."

Berkeley was released from prison on June 20, 1865, and returned home. He was a tutor and school teacher in Loudoun, Orange, and Madison counties until his retirement in 1904. Henry married his cousin Anna Louisa Berkeley on August 8, 1883, and they had one son. Berkeley died in Orange on January 16, 1918.

CHARLES BRANDEGEE

Private Charles Brandegee was imprisoned initially at Camp Sumter near Andersonville, Georgia. When that prison was closed, he was transferred to a camp at Florence, South Carolina, in October 1864. Shortly after his arrival there, he wrote to his father:

"I am in good health and spirits, and hope the time will come when I can see you."

He was finally released from prison in February 1865, and traveled home to recover his health. He is said to have weighed only ninety pounds when he reached his family. In April, Charles Brandegee was well enough to go to New York City. There he was discharged from the United States army the following month.

After the war, Brandegee and a brother helped establish Greely, Colorado. He next worked as a cattleman and county clerk until his return to the east in 1894. He lived in Farmington, Connecticut, and became town clerk and probate court judge. When he retired in 1925, he moved to Somerville, Massachusetts. On August 12, 1886, Brandegee had married Mabel Daggett, and they had one daughter. He died on September 22, 1927, of a cerebral hemorrhage and was buried in Mt. Auburn Cemetery, in Cambridge, Massachusetts.

WILLIAM BULL

"But we want to leave here and go into the field again. We are anxious to go into Missouri and wake up the Feds once more. We are not as sick of this War as they think we are. We can fight them two or three years longer just as well as not. The only trouble is we don't like to be kept from home so long."

"...My first object, as a soldier, is to serve my country to the best of my ability. My second is to have as easy a time as possible (I imagine I hear you laugh and call me lazy—well, I plead guilty to the charge). ..."

" We are in camp here and expect to remain for some time. Have no fears for the success of the South. <u>She will be free</u>. I never have, for one moment, regretted having come here, and am now, as I always have been, determined to remain until that which I come to assist in accomplishing <u>has been accomplished</u>."

Bull was on furlough when the Trans-Mississippi army surrendered in June 1865. He soon returned home to St. Louis. Bull was Inspector General of Missouri for eight years and spent most of his life in the insurance business in St. Louis. He died of heart disease while on vacation in Miami, Florida, on January 8, 1928. His body was brought back to St. Louis and was buried in Bellefontaine Cemetery.

Corporal Elisha Stockwell, Jr.

From Byron R. Abernathy (ed.), <u>Private Stockwell, Jr. Sees the Civil War</u> (Norman: University of Oklahoma Press, 1958).

VALERIUS CINCINNATUS GILES

Valerius C. Giles was captured on October 28, 1863, in an engagement at Wauhatchie, Tennessee. He was imprisoned at Camp Morton, at Indianapolis, Indiana. On November 8, 1864, he and a comrade escaped.

"Jack's idea was to go to some town, find some fellow with more money than patriotism, hire out to him as a substitute, and, at the first good opportunity, light out and travel like gentlemen. To this hazardous proposition I would not agree."

"I was hiding out and dodging through the country as an escaped prisoner of war, and I was not going to add disgrace to my unpleasant position by deserting the Confederacy and joining the Yankee army. That was a little more than I could stand, and I told Jack emphatically that I would not go with him."

Giles made his way to northern Kentucky and joined a force commanded by Major Walker Taylor, who was there recruiting men for the Confederate army. He fought with Taylor until the end of the war. He received his final parole at Louisville in mid-April 1865.

After the war, Giles worked in the General Land Office in Austin. He married Lou Barnhart in 1873, and they had two children. Giles died on January 31, 1915.

GEORGE JOB HUNTLEY

The vast majority of Confederate soldiers refused to desert, even when the war was clearly going against them. What were some of the reasons involved in their decision? Desertion

Sergeant Peter Welsh.

Courtesy Collection of the New-York
Historical Society, New York.

would have meant abandoning their comrades, to whom most soldiers felt a debt of loyalty from their shared military experience. The Christian ethic also kept Confederates in the ranks. They did not see defeat as a repudiation of their government or cause, but as weakness in themselves. These soldiers kept fighting to seek God's favor. Racial solidarity played a part in Confederates' continuing loyalty. Many recoiled at the prospect of social and economic equality of the races. Finally, the threat of continued Yankee domination motivated these men to keep on. Even after two or more years of marching and fighting, the many hardships and dangers they had faced, and the loss of comrades in battle or to disease, most Civil War soldiers on both sides kept the faith, and maintained their commitment.

ELI PINSON LANDERS

Private Eli Pinson Landers fought with his regiment in the Battle of Chickamauga, Georgia, on September 19-20, 1863. While marching toward the battlefield, he was tempted to leave the ranks and visit his family:

"Dear Mother, I tell you it was a trying case for me to pass so near home and not call, but I...thought it was my duty to stick to the company, deny myself, forsake home for the present, and cleave to the cause of our bleeding country to drive the oppressors from our soil....I expect to be a man of honor to our country, at the risk of my life. I don't want to be a disgrace to myself nor my relations."

While stationed near Chattanooga, Tennessee, Landers became ill and was taken to a hospital. He died of typhoid fever on October 27, 1863, while at Rome, Georgia. Several weeks before, he had written his mother:

"I reckon you will hear that I am very sick and I have been but I am getting better....I was afraid that some of the boys would write that I was very sick but I am a heap better—most well, so don't be uneasy."

DELAVAN S. MILLER

"A serious problem faced the government in 1863, for within a few months it would lose the services of its veteran soldiers because their enlistments would end. A bargain was made to the three-years men that if they would re-enlist, they would receive four hundred-two dollars bounty and a thirty-day furlough. The bargain was accepted by a majority of the old soldiers, and the old regiments were kept with their officers."

"Most of our company and regiment re-enlisted. They sent us home in squads, and when it came my turn, I was laid up with the mumps and could not go with my father."

"While I was finally in the north on my furlough,...[m]y father wrote me that our regiment had received orders to be ready to go to the front at an hour's notice."

"My furlough had several days to run, but I took the first train for Washington, and in twenty-four hours walked into camp."

"I found our regiment all ready and awaiting orders. Field tents, rubber blankets, and other things were issued to us, which indicated that we were to take the field."

Miller was mustered out of the army on September 29, 1865, and returned home. He became a clerk and bookkeeper at Carthage and Watertown, New York. Miller married Luella Georgiana Rhiner on May 11, 1868, at Hewelton, New York, and they had four children. He suffered from injuries sustained during the war and illnesses that had afflicted him. Frequently his ailments prevented him from working. Miller died on July 26, 1917, at Watertown.

ALEXANDER HERRITAGE NEWTON

"...We had been promised fifteen dollars bounty on our enlistment, but...no effort, it seems, had been made to pay us this money....We had long been accustomed to such impositions; but we said that we would honor Old Glory, obey God, and contend for our prize—Liberty—... until the sound of clanking slave chains shall be heard no more in the length and breadth of this fair and goodly land."

"…When we were told…that we could receive only seven dollars per month each for our services, our spirits fell….The officers advised us to take it, and assured us that at the next payment we should receive our full compensation….We quieted our passions and went to work like good soldiers. My great desire was to get into contact with the Southern forces that we might be working out the decision of this great problem….I had no ill feeling for the Southern white people—some of them had been my best friends—but this was not a personal matter, but a question of national issue, involving the welfare of millions, and my soul was on fire for the question: Slavery or No Slavery? to be forever settled, and that too as soon as possible."

Newton was mustered out of service on November 25, 1865. He became a preacher in the African Methodist Episcopal

Lieutenant William
Marcus Woodcock.

Courtesy of Mrs. Martha Teschan,
Nashville, Tennessee.

Church and served churches in Tennessee, Arkansas, Louisiana, North Carolina, and New Jersey. Newton's first wife died in 1868, and he married Lula L. Campbell on June 1, 1876. They had four children. Newton died of heart problems on April 29, 1921, in Camden, New Jersey.

WILLIAM CHARLES HENRY REEDER

William Reeder refused to re-enlist for another three-year term.

"I will not sell myself for three years to get a thirty-days furlough and...a few paltry dollars. Those that are coming for the money, now is the time let them pitch in....I think this: if I serve my three years and the war is not closed, then let some other young, stout man come in my place and try it awhile. I do actually feel today as if I had, since I come out, had ten years added to me: the service is very hard on a man or beast. And then, this war has turned out very different from what I thought it would in my mind,...and I do not propose to fight any more in such a cause if I can avoid it."

Like many of his comrades, Reeder opposed the Emancipation Proclamation and the enlistment of black soldiers. Most white Union soldiers were not fighting to free the slaves, and many doubted the fighting abilities of blacks. After black units proved themselves in battle, most whites realized these thousands of new soldiers would help bring the war to a swifter conclusion.

After leaving the army in July 1864, Reeder returned to Peru and worked as a cabinet maker. Two years later he became a pattern builder in the wood department of a local railroad company. He married Agnes Catherine Weist on October 21, 1869, and they had seven children. Agnes died in 1902, and two years later Reeder married Martha Weist. He died in Peru on October 5, 1932.

ELISHA STOCKWELL, JR.

"We re-enlisted here in the latter part of December, 1863, for three years or during the war. But as I hadn't been in two years, I couldn't re-enlist until my two years were up. But I promised to re-enlist. We were to get three hundred dollars and a thirty-day furlough, so I went home with the regiment. The furlough was the big inducement."

"...One day [during my furlough, I was in a bar] sitting by the stove, when a man came in,...and he finally came and sat by me. He asked me if I knew what I was fighting for. I told him that I didn't care to talk politics—wasn't posted in that line. He told me how the South was being abused, that we never could whip them, and finally said he would bet I couldn't tell him what I was fighting for. I told him I was fighting to whip just such men as he was, and I would think more of him if he would take a gun and go down there and help them."

While on leave, Elisha Stockwell married Katherine Hurley of Milwaukee on March 14, 1864.

Stockwell was mustered out of the army on October 9, 1865. He and his wife eventually had eleven children. They lived in Alma, Wisconsin, until 1872, and moved then to Otter Tail County, Minnesota. Four years later, the Stockwells moved to a farm near Black River Falls, Wisconsin. In 1906, they moved to Beach, North Dakota. Stockwell died of endocarditis on December 29, 1935, and was buried in the Beach Cemetery.

PETER WELSH

In the Union armies, patriotism and idealism remained strong for many soldiers despite the reverses they suffered, even when it seemed the conflict would continue for years. Though weary of war, they were determined to keep fighting for the ideals of freedom and liberty. Some were seeking revenge for their dead and maimed countrymen. Others wanted to punish the people they saw as traitors. As with the Confederates, loyalty to their comrades kept some Union soldiers in the ranks through the darkest days of the war.

Even after two or more years of marching and fighting, the many hardships and dangers they had faced, and the loss of comrades in battle or to disease, most Civil War soldiers on both sides kept the faith, and maintained their commitment.

WILLIAM MARCUS WOODCOCK

"We have grown too proud—have come to the conclusion that we are wiser, better, and more patriotic than our illustrious ancestors....Thousands are to be found in this bloodbought land who openly scout the greatest principles that Washington and our other great government makers advocated with a tenacity exceeding life. The emotions of love and patriotism that once filled so many bosoms at the mention of American honor and glory are now unknown to millions of those who have been most favored by the great institutions of this glorious country, and these millions are now at open war with the government—and that to preserve the most abominable institution that ever stained the bright escutcheon of our country."

"Yes, they are waging a most terrible and bloody war, which is costing our country the lives of thousands of patriots and millions of treasure that they may enslave an unfortunate race, which is decreed by heaven shall be free. But we will come victorious out of this struggle, and if our country's history is stained with the black spot of one civil war, it will be the brighter by the removal of the blacker one of slavery."

Woodcock was mustered out of the army on December 15, 1864, at the expiration of his enlistment. He became a member of the Tennessee legislature and served two terms. Woodcock married Ellen Waters in 1868. After leaving the legislature, he held various business and political jobs. Woodcock died in Nashville in February 1914.

Overall, soldiers on both sides were driven by a belief in their cause and a sense of duty to their comrades, country and community. That commitment helped them to endure the hardships of a soldier's life and enabled them to shape the history of this nation. It is their willingness to sacrifice that transformed their lives, and it is for that sacrifice, the extraordinary efforts of ordinary American citizens in extreme circumstances, that Pamplin Historical Park honors them.

BIBLIOGRAPHY

Sources for Soldier Comrades

Abernathy, Byron R., ed. *Private Stockwell, Jr. Sees the Civil War.* Norman: University of Oklahoma Press, 1958.

Banasik, Michael E., ed. *Missouri Brothers in Gray: The Reminiscences and Letters of William J. Bull and John P. Bull.* Iowa City: Press of the Camp Pope Bookshop, 1998.

Kohl, Lawrence F. (ed.). *Irish Green & Union Blue: The Civil War Letters of Peter Welsh, Color Sergeant, 28th Massachusetts Volunteers.* New York: Fordham University Press, 1986.

Lasswell, Mary (comp. and ed.). *Rags and Hope: The Recollections of Val C. Giles, Four Years with Hood's Brigade, Fourth Texas Infantry, 1861-1865.* New York: Coward McCann, 1961.

Livingstone, Charles Brandegee (ed.). *Charlie's Civil War: A Private's Trial by Fire in the 5th New York Volunteers—Duryée Zouaves and 146th New York Volunteer Infantry.* Gettsyburg, Pa.: Thomas Publications, 1997.

Miller, Delavan S. *Drum Taps in Dixie: Memories of a Drummer Boy, 1861-1865.* Watertown, N. Y.: Hungerford-Holbrook Co., 1905.

Newton, Alexander H. *Out of the Briars: An Autobiography and Sketch of the Twenty-ninth Regiment, Connecticut Volunteers.* Philadelphia: The A. M. E. Book Concern, 1910; reprint ed., Miami, Fla.: Mnemosyne Pub. Co., 1969.

Noe, Kenneth W., ed. *A Southern Boy in Blue: The Memoir of Marcus Woodcock, 9th Kentucky Infantry (U. S. A.).* Knoxville: University of Tennessee Press, 1996.

Reeder, William C. H., Papers. United States Army Military History Institute Archives, Carlisle Barracks, Pa.

Roberson, Elizabeth W. (ed.). *In Care of Yellow River: The Complete Civil War Letters of Pvt. Eli Pinson Landers to His Mother.* Gretna, La.: Pelican Publishing Co., 1997.

Runge, William H., ed. *Four Years in the Confederate Artillery: The Diary of Private Henry Robinson Berkeley.* Chapel Hill: University of North Carolina Press, 1961; reprint ed., Richmond: Virginia Historical Society, 1991.

Taylor, Michael W. (ed.). *The Cry is War, War, War: The Civil War Correspondence of Lts. Burwell Thomas Cotton and George Job Huntley, 34th Regiment North Carolina Troops, Pender-Scales Brigade of the Light Division, Stonewall Jackson's and A. P. Hill's Corps, Army of Northern Virginia, CSA.* Dayton, Ohio: Morningside House, Inc., 1994.

Vanderslice, Catherine H., ed. *The Civil War Letters of George Washington Beidelman.* New York: Vantage Press, 1978.

General Works on the Common Soldier

Barton, Michael. *Goodmen: The Character of Civil War Soldiers.* University Park: Pennsylvania State University Press, 1981.

Billings, John D. *Hard Tack and Coffee: The Unwritten Story of Army Life.* Williamstown: Corner House Publishers, 1993.

Daniel, Larry J. *Soldiering in the Army of Tennessee: A Portrait of Life in the Confederate Army.* Chapel Hill: University of North Carolina Press, 1991.

Frank, Joseph Allan, and George A. Reaves. *"Seeing the Elephant:" Raw Recruits at the Battle of Shiloh.* Westport, Conn.: Greenwood Press, 1989.

Glatthaar, Joseph T. *Forged in Battle: The Civil War Alliance of Black Soldiers and White Officers.* New York: The Free Press, 1990.

Hess, Earl J. *The Union Soldier in Battle: Enduring the Ordeal of Combat.* Lawrence: University Press of Kansas, 1997.

Linderman, Gerald F. *Embattled Courage: The Experience of Combat in the American Civil War*. New York: The Free Press, 1987.

McCarthy, Carlton. *Detailed Minutiae of Soldier Life in the Army of Northern Virginia, 1861-1865*. Richmond, Va.: Carlton McCarthy and Company, 1882; reprint ed., Lincoln: University of Nebraska Press, 1993.

McPherson, James M. *For Cause and Comrades: Why Men Fought in the Civil War*. New York: Oxford University Press, 1997.

McPherson, James M. *What They Fought For, 1861-1865*. Baton Rouge: Louisiana State University Press, 1994.

Mitchell, Reid. *Civil War Soldiers: Their Expectations and Their Experiences*. New York: Viking Penquin, Inc., 1988.

Power, J. Tracy. *Lee's Miserables: Life in the Army of Northern Virginia from the Wilderness to Appomattox*. Chapel Hill: University of North Carolina Press, 1998.

Robertson, James I., Jr. *Soldiers Blue and Gray*. Columbia: University of South Carolina Press, 1988.

Wiley, Bell I. *The Life of Billy Yank: The Common Soldier of the Union*. Reprint ed., Baton Rouge: Louisiana State University Press, 1978.

Wiley, Bell I. *The Life of Johnny Reb: The Common Soldier of the Confederacy*. Reprint ed., Baton Rouge: Louisiana State University Press, 1978.